I0796390

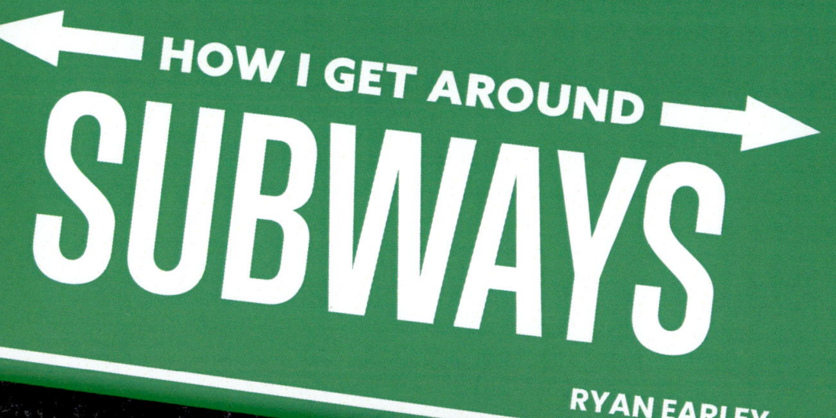

TABLE OF CONTENTS

A Pelican Book

Teaching Tips for Caregivers and Teachers:

Research shows that one of the best ways for students to learn a new topic is to read about it.

Before Reading

- Read the title and predict what the book will be about.
- Read the "Words to Know" and discuss the meaning of each word.
- Read the back cover to see what the book is about.

During Reading

- When a student gets to a word that is unknown, ask them to look at the rest of the sentence to find clues to help with the meaning of the unknown word.
- Motivate students with praise and encouragement.

After Reading

- Discuss the main idea of the book.
- Ask students to give one detail that they learned in the book.

Sight Words

all	get	I
around	go	many
by	have	on

Words to Know

cars

engines

subway

tracks

underground

wheels

I get around by **subway**.

subway
033
Ealing Broadway
District line
21402

All subways have **engines**.

engine
СЯ-Е

All subways have many **cars**.

cars

wheel

All subway cars have **wheels.**

All subways go on **tracks**.

tracks

All subways go **underground**.

underground

Index

Written by: Ryan Earley
Design by: Niko Magaro
Editor: Kim Thompson
Series Development: James Earley

Photos: All images from Shutterstock

Library of Congress PCN Data
Subways / Ryan Earley
How I Get Around
ISBN 979-8-8945-9255-8(hard cover)
ISBN 979-8-8945-9269-5(paperback)
ISBN 979-8-8945-9297-8(EPUB)
ISBN 979-8-8945-9283-1(eBook)
ISBN 979-8-8945-9311-1(audio)
ISBN 979-8-8945-9325-8(Read-Along)
Library of Congress Control Number: 2024946358

Printed in Canada/012025/CP20250101

Seahorse Publishing Company
seahorsepub.com

Published in the United States
Seahorse Publishing
PO Box 771325
Coral Springs, FL 33077